BUSINESS/SCIENCE/TECHNOLOGY DIVISION
CHICAGO PUBLIC LIBRARY
400 SOUTH STATE STREET
CHICAGO, IL 60605

DISCARD

REFERENCE DEPARTMENT
CHICAGO PUBLIC LIBRARY
400 SOUTH STATE STREET
CHICAGO, IL 60605

R01196 32831

BUSINESS/SCIENCE/TECHNOLOGY DIVISION
CHICAGO PUBLIC LIBRARY
400 SOUTH STATE STREET
CHICAGO, IL 60605

Allen G. Viduka

PENTLAND PRESS, INC.
ENGLAND • USA • SCOTLAND

PUBLISHED BY PENTLAND PRESS, INC.
5124 Bur Oak Circle, Raleigh, North Carolina 27612
United States of America
919-782-0281

ISBN 1-57197-073-8
Library of Congress Catalog Card Number 97-67135

Copyright © 1997 Allen Gene Viduka
All rights reserved, which includes the right to reproduce this book
or portions thereof in any form whatsoever except as provided by
the U.S. Copyright Law.

Printed in the United States of America

DEDICATION

This book is dedicated to four things. The first is the memory of the 1987 and 1991 Minnesota Twins. Although their story did not survive the final edit of this book, their struggle and success had more to do with the stubborn optimism I clung to during my naval career than any other factor. To Kirby Puckett, Kent Hrbek, Gary Gaetti, Tom Brunansky and the whole gang: you picked me up during the lowest and hardest moments of my life. It is only fitting that I pay tribute to what you helped me accomplish in my life.

Second, this book is dedicated to hope and vision of the *Star Trek* universe. I tried to dedicate lines of poetry to this positive force in my life but these lines were myopically and regretfully deemed unacceptable. The fictional Commander Data is the one being that I can sympathize with more than any other. I hope that one day the human race will accept the "Data's" of our world as true, sentient citizens capable of enriching humanity. To William Shatner: I have walked in your footsteps, Sir. Whether you realize it or not, Mr. Shatner, you have helped a great many of us to take that first step away from this singular planet and towards a glorious universe of endless diversity and hope. My dream is of a humanity spread across the universe. Star Trek helped foster that dream not just in my heart but in the collective soul of humanity.

Third, I dedicate this book to my friends all across the globe. Thomas Palmer, David Raffo, Chris Miller, James Ziolkowkski, Robert Insall, Dale Magargee, Dan Leathers, Joseph Kurensky, John Nigro, Paul Johnson Donald Howell and Kevin Weimert and countless others, I hope that you will see that, although I'm a crazy dreamer, I'm still your friend. Let us put the past behind us and concentrate on building a better tomorrow. I offer each of you my gratitude for your time and camaraderie. Although all I have is memories of our friendship, I treasure them.

Finally, this book is dedicated to the naval career I left behind. Given the time, I might have become the best Sonar Technician possible, but that opportunity was cut short before I could reach out and use the skills the Navy was kind enough to let me learn. To this day, I know the Soviet submarine fleet well because of my training. If it hadn't been for the brick wall that severed my hopes of a life-long career in the Navy, I would have become the veteran I know I could have been. Although I seemed to fail in my naval career, I still hold the entire United States Navy in the highest esteem. I hope that those servicemen will join with me to help build the future.

To all who will read this book: thank you and God speed!

a. g. v.

TABLE OF CONTENTS

INTRODUCTION

Writing a book on schizophrenia is the only way I know to get at the heart of what people diagnosed with this disorder—people like me—suffer on a regular basis. I experienced a schizophrenic disorder during a religious war against Saddam Hussein in the Persian Gulf. The illness was like a virus I had to fight in stages. Its seeds were sown far before I went to the Gulf, but, as is often the case with schizophrenia, the disease needed one traumatic experience to set it off. I could have been called "the king of the paranoid" for my perspective, believing as I did that a second American Civil War was going on around me. But there was always a logical, rational individual guiding me at the core of who I was out there. I suffered a breakdown under those difficult conditions, and I need to put some closure on that part of my life. I cannot let this disease pull me under the waves. I wanted to write this book as a way of forging my path back from the brink.

Today, with proper medication and an outlook firmly grounded in reality, I've found that I can no longer let this disease sit on the shelf. There are many people in this country who suffer from mental illness, and only a few of us are getting the treatment we need. Also, many times in the past, those in the medical community have fed me false information about my condition. I hope this book will be informative and helpful to doctors, psychiatrists, social workers, and other schizophrenics who have suffered as I have.

I've seen and experienced many different stages of schizophrenia, and taken note of the reactions of others with this disorder. One thing I've found about schizophrenics is that they do less acting than the rest of the human race. Their behavior is more real to them than reality. If they believe something is happening, it actually is—to them. I've suffered through many shades of schizophrenia, many illusions and delusions, so I know.

The illness I went through also makes good drama—another reason I feel I should write about it. Picture a person, one month a decorated hero for saving his ship from a flooding casualty, the next, an outcast because of the choices he made in dealing with his illness, choices that included peeling back multiple layers of rationality to get to his core, where he found that he believed more strongly in idealism than in saving his military career. I couldn't allow myself to ruin my personal dream of a world where money is no longer the guiding force, where ideas and ideals run wild, where everyone can make a difference, where education is available to all, where "survival" becomes a word for astronauts instead of self-styled militias and those who fear nuclear war, and where people who were once the closest friends can overcome the stigma of schizophrenia and regain their friendship.

I hope this book seems well-rounded. Regardless of how much effort I put into it, there are likely to be points both large and small that I couldn't remember and therefore left out. Time and the winds of history are things of nostalgia, and if I don't capture an idea the instant it takes flight, it is often lost in the void.

Please read this book with some empathy for a writer and person who isn't the stuff of legends, but just a mixed-up individual trying to anchor himself in the physical, emotional, and spiritual planes of this planet all at once. Should I lose my dreams because I suffer from a disorder of the mind? Should I not rebuild my castle on the same site to emphasize that I won't allow this disease to ravage me anymore? Am I on the cutting edge of determining what healthy thought is and what it isn't? I don't know, but I'd rather be out here in the conceptual wilderness than grappling with the overwhelming, mundane concerns of existence. At least here I can make a difference, and that's what counts.

Allen G. Viduka

WHAT WILL HAPPEN WHEN THE BOOK GETS PUBLISHED?

How will the common man react
when he hears of a paranoia
so thick you can slice it
with a knife?

How will the common man react
when faced with one man's Civil War?
Within a schizophrenic mind,
the armies of North and South battle again.

How will the common man react
to a messenger saying World War III
is one delusion the world can't shake
no matter how hard it tries?

How will the artist react?
Will it skew his or her vision?
Will they act like I'm deranged
because I believed my mind's eye?

How will the writer react?
Will this story be ignored
or will I hear it as a parable
recounted time and time again?

How will the researcher react?
Can I egg them on to a cure?
Will textbooks be written
that prevent the Republican/Democratic schizophrenia
from drying up funding
for one of the worst illnesses of the mind?

How will the Pentagon react?
Will there be revolution in the ranks?
Will there be martial law because the president is powerless
to stop a schizophrenic soul
who writes himself into a cure?

How will religions react?
Will this ignite a holy war
or will they say I'm just delusional
and order this book to be burned?

How will the paranoid person react
and the sons and daughters of the Confederate revolution?
Will we all wrap ourselves in the flag
and point the cannon at Saddam and me
while the super-patriots cringe in disgust?
And will the wheels of the Republic continue to rust?

How will the reader react
to a victim of total honesty?
Do I seek an impossible dream?
To gain a real friend—
is it too much to ask?
Will I have to be at war forever?

BEFORE THE ILLNESS . . .

THE LONELY YEARS

My unique journey through life has been filled with periods of prolonged isolationism. During high school, this isolationism and my inability to "fit in" set me apart from the rest of the crowd. I developed an outlook that is far different from believing that life should be one big beer-guzzling party. I believe my high school experiences made me the strong-willed individual I am today. I think of this period as the start of my split from a conventional outlook on life.

My high school days were spent in silent contemplation of events around me. I was a runner on the cross-country team for four years, and read books (mostly science fiction) in my spare time. While I do not remember much about what I was doing on any particular day, I do remember that I made a conscious choice to not attend the prom, graduation proceedings, or any other social event. I did not want to waste my valuable free time by searching for the ever-elusive quality known as popularity. It is true that if I had gone on more dates in high school, or if I had more interaction with members of the opposite sex, I probably would have had a less-severe break from my isolationism when I joined the military and the typical young enlisted men's drinking circle.

The days of my military enlistment were filled with adventure; we sailors had an endless string of one-night stands, with a girl in every port. To say that I was trying to live every moment to its fullest, to make up for time lost during my high school days, would be an understatement. But I'm not here to talk about my conquests as a sailor. Even with all the womanizing I did, I never broke out of my isolationism. I have never formed a romantic relationship with a woman that has lasted more than a couple of weeks.

I have a deep void in my heart that may never be filled. I may always be alone, and never get the chance to share my triumphs and my love for nature with another person. I do not wish this to happen, but I feel it is an ever-growing possibility that I will never find true love. I do not know what the future will bring for me, but I do believe in the romanticism of past eras. This is another thing that has always set me apart from the current generation of men; I do not know what decade I belong in, or what century. My strongest held beliefs do set me apart from the modern, technology-driven society that we live in. My struggle against isolation is still a central issue in my life. I must attempt to break the cycle of self-imposed isolation that affected my early formative years.

THE POSMO CADET

Boot Camp Experiences

Few times have I shown more courage than when I was a student at the Positive Motivation clinic in boot camp. "POSMO" is the term used by boot camp participants to indicate a special company designed for those who, for whatever reason, had trouble with some part of the boot camp experience. These were people who either had trouble with rifle drills, some form of military instruction or activities such as folding their clothes properly, or had to be disciplined more often than their peers—this included being sent to Marching Party and Shore Tour. POSMO cadets were, in general, military "screw-ups" who were sent to this special school to derive some positive motivation towards finishing boot camp.

I was sent to Marching Party on seven occasions over breaches in military protocol, and I always mystified my commanders (and gained some respect from them) by coming back with a passing grade. Marching Party was a series of exercises, and either a "pass" or "fail" label was recorded. It was a way of weeding out the "undesirables" and those who had no endurance; additional physical training could be given to recruits after the workday had ended. Cadets did jumping jacks, pushups, sit-ups and leg-ups, eight-count exercises, and a lot of running in place; we viewed these exercises as punishment.

Endurance in physical punishment was a trait I'd learned while running cross-country in high school, and I actually lived for the moments when I could dedicate some time to proving that I could do something right. I believed that I could do anything if I dedicated myself to the challenge. My endurance would serve me well for much of my early enlisted life. I began to think of Marching Party as an afternoon jog in the park, and would brag to my shipmates about my stamina. Marching Parties were fairly standard, but a couple of episodes stand out in my mind.

The first was a Marching Party where the instructor was getting peeved because so many recruits were being sent home after they failed the program. He ordered all the remaining survivors to "get up off their asses" and prepare to run the grinder—a large piece of open ground reserved for marching in ranks and training the "rubber-necks," as we were called. Running the grinder is an experience that no cadet will ever forget. In this case, all the members of the Marching Party were ordered to run around the grinder and then reassemble in ranks for more exercise.

Another time, the instructor had been pushing us hard for over one hour in exercise, when taps sounded (indicating lights out). The instructor made us do a few more pushups, then said to the sweaty, dirty lot of us, "I don't want to hear a sound out of any of you, or we're all going to come back and do it again tomorrow." The group broke up at that point, like a flock of birds who were suddenly released. We quickly ran across the grinder and scattered to our various barracks.

Shore Tour was a step up from the physical training of the Marching Party. A new element was added to the training; each participant was issued a (non-firing) M-1 rifle, and the rifle added a new degree of misery to the proceedings. Now, the instructor could make everyone do exercises with or without the rifle. He could order us to hold it out in front of us (at arms' length) while jogging in place, or we could be forced to hold it over our heads. We could be ordered to do military drills with the rifle, or run the grinder while holding it over our heads.

Shore Tour was a period of exercise that was not for the faint of heart; it was a grueling period of military punishment and exercise that took every ounce of strength out of you. It separated the men from the boys. If you survived Shore Tour, you could wear it like a badge of honor. The motto around boot camp was "Stay out of Shore Tour," but I was sent to it on two occasions and passed both times.

The POSMO unit gathered all the hard-luck candidates into one company. We came from both drill and infantry companies, but the common factor was that we didn't fit into the shows our commanders were trying to run, for whatever reason, so we were sent to POSMO to await reassignment to another unit. I arrived at POSMO and got settled in; I took my gear from the heavy sea bag I had been forced to carry on my back for a full mile. POSMO was like a period of peace and quiet after my run-ins with certain commanders. I exchanged stories with the other cadets to learn why each had been sent there, and to determine what we could do to make our "second chance" a success.

While at POSMO, we spent each day in instruction, learning what we had to do in order to act as responsible recruits. The company commander taught us everything we needed to make it through boot camp. POSMO was a place where time seemed to stand still; each recruit sent there got to enter a new company after completing the program. We were simply biding time in POSMO until a new company was chosen to continue our training. On the day I left POSMO, I was summoned by the commanding officer. He told me that I had earned my second chance, and it was going to be my last one. In parting, he told me specifically not to "screw it up." I had every intention of doing what he directed. I was now on a personal quest to pole-vault myself from boot camp and into the new world (whatever lay beyond boot camp).

As I look back on POSMO and boot camp, I see them as places where stories and memories were made. Surviving the various programs could be hell or the highlight of a lifetime; for me, it was both. I relate these incidents because I'm only human, and I have drawbacks like everyone else on this planet. Life experience has made me unique in many respects; I can excel in some areas, yet fail miserably in others. This has shown me that there are many sides to every issue, and surface appearances can be misleading. During all my years in the military, I never really understood how the chain of command worked. I did the best I could and stayed dedicated to living one day at a time, trying to enjoy the moments as they came. It was only later that paranoia grabbed my mind and truly divorced me from the military, once and for all.

HURRICANE HUGO

My Impressions

Hurricane Hugo hit Charleston, South Carolina, while I was attending the Fleet Mine Warfare School there. What I remember most is the immense, damaging winds that accompanied the storm. I was in the barracks (enlisted residential quarters) at the time. I recollect that at the height of the storm, a tremendous wind broke every glass window in the barracks. I recall quite succinctly the pandemonium around me as our auxiliary power system came on. People screamed in the hallways as the wind knocked out window after window. We had been instructed to form an "X" on each window with masking tape to cut down on broken glass, but this did not seem to help much. So many windows were cracked and shattered, it was as if we hadn't taken any preventative measures.

As the wind howled fiercely, the commanding officer of the barracks told us to vacate our building and move to safer quarters (another barracks in the row closest to ours). We fled with our pillows and mattresses. Due to the ninety-mile-an-hour winds, we had a hard time running the distance to the safe haven, less than thirty yards away.

Charleston was hit by the front and rear edges of the hurricane. We also passed through the eye of the storm; this quiet period seemed like a tranquil summer day, even though the hurricane had already caused massive amounts of damage.

I remained safe during the storm, but once the devastation of that night had passed, I got out bright and early to survey the damage to the local naval base. I found telephone poles lying cracked and broken at odd angles in the street. The base's traffic lights were busted; some had been blown away by the wind. Live power lines were lying across every sidewalk. Near a dockside pier, a barge weighing over one ton had been tipped upside down. Branches and tree limbs were everywhere, and a wooden-hulled minesweeper suffered damage below the waterline. When I approached my school's command building, the pronounced devastation wreaked by the storm became apparent.

The Fleet Mine Warfare schoolhouse was a two-story brick building, and one whole wall was destroyed. The roof of the building had collapsed; there was massive damage to all the equipment inside. Every deserted corridor had up to an inch of standing water. Every ceiling tile was ruined, as well as every computer and unsecured file. The building became a dark labyrinth of hallways, lit only by workers wearing lighted hard-hats or by portable lanterns. Members of the base command worked fifteen-hour shifts in order to clean up the damage. Luckily, the base itself was not inundated with several feet of floodwaters from the Charleston River, as was expected.

While exploring the building, I came across an office with a storm-tracking photo secured to the side of a cabinet. The photo was dotted by stickpins, which tracked the hurricane from the Atlantic Ocean into Charleston. I was struck by the absence of the very last pin, which would have been the point where the storm hit Charleston. Apparently, the person tracking the hurricane became so busy that he could not finish his diagram, which lay abandoned in the Fleet Mine Warfare building.

I did not survey downtown Charleston until two weeks after the storm, but I was kept updated on the cleanup efforts by photos in the local newspaper. Historic Charleston was a mess; many landmarks suffered damage, and the local attractions, theme parks, and the national park at Fort Sumter were all closed for much of the season. It took several months for Charleston to recover from this storm, the worst to hit the area in several decades.

Most of the United States Navy ships that were docked at Charleston's base left for the Atlantic up to one week before the storm. A mass exodus over a three-day period signaled to those of us unlucky enough to stay in Charleston that there was a good chance the storm would hit us. Those ships that, for whatever reason, couldn't make it out of Charleston set up hurricane-docking schemes with their ropes to ride out the storm.

The hurricane I witnessed in Charleston will always be remembered as part of my service in the military. A hurricane is an awesome, destructive force, and should not be ignored. Hurricane Hugo left such a scene of devastation that I cannot forget it, because it left a lasting imprint on my mind.

PURGATORY

ON THE EDGE OF REALITY

When I first met the Writer I was just returning from a foreign war, still trying to shake the rhetoric of a dictator, a flood of insanity that ran against the current in a pool of fully grown fish. The Writer was an expression of the symbolism of our times. He was a man possessed with a keen eye and acute intuition about the people, places, and things around him. He knew all the ins and outs of writing, and could turn a phrase, wrap it around his finger, or spin it like a bottle, then stop it like a wheel of fortune without ever losing the bet. To his detriment, he was a man who lived alone, and also an environmentalist. When I met him in the Philippines, we struck up a friendship that has since stood the test of time. We needed each other, like a plant needs soil to grow or a flower needs sunlight to bloom. Without the Writer, I never would have reached maturity, and I may have lost all rationality as I struggled to deal with a dictator's hatred on seas that a navy could sail but could rule only briefly in the DNA strand of time that is this century.

The Writer told me of the land he'd come from, a land I still dream of to this day. He called it "the Republic," a realm far different from anything I'd experienced, and its tale still fires my soul. He spoke of a land where the government cares for the poor and the sick, where everyone has a job and an ambition, and where ideals are common to the king, the poet, the Lyricist, the artist, and even the practical man. There the elderly live in splendid cottages by crystal-clear lakes so pristine that painters and their apprentices set up canvases to capture the beautiful views. In this land the deficit is as ancient as the dinosaurs, and even the lowest born can have pride of place. There are no diseases of the body, mind, or spirit, nor are there currencies or insurance agencies. Education is free to all, so people can better themselves instead of merely surviving. Precious metals are no longer a cause of war in this land, all of the vehicles are powered by the sun, and mankind is reaching out to explore the stars.

As I listened, I had a tear in my eye. I could hardly think, and the revolution proposed by the dictator slowly disappeared from my mind to be replaced by an idealism so strong that hurricane winds could neither blow it away nor wreck it.

The Writer, on his end, became a poet by listening to my account of the purgatorial fires unleashed in our age in our land. I told him of a time when the intensities of living dragged a man's spirit down, and the exploration of the mind in eternal conflict was the illusion of truth. I explained faith to him, and the million-to-one dream. I could tell afterward that I'd had an effect, because he paused, then told me my spirit was true. "Comrade," he said, "I've seen the unknown, and you've got nothing to fear. Whether you live or die, the eternal will always be near."

We paused in our conversation and looked up. With a roar, the machines of war passed over us, streaking by at the speed of sound. Fireflies quietly gathered at the edge of runways for their one-way trip into history books, while missiles flew overhead with the photographic fantasy of modern war. A bird sang, and petrol burned on the sea. Somewhere in the distance, tracers flew into the darkness, and a scudding site lit up the night with an eerie light.

Now that our paths have crossed, I cannot shut the Writer out of my life. Our dreams have been shared and intermingled. He's my best friend, and I cannot let him down. He shared the dreams of his vision, and I shared the reality of mine. We're stronger for it now, and the past seems to have started a new future, one where two men can write an epic of history for a wider audience than ever before.

COLD WAR EMBERS

Fires burn till this day
I can't put them out
I don't know how
nor was I asked
to think of a solution
to this conflict

In our day we were titans
raging against one another
burning bridges, schools, homes
the one common feeling we possessed
anger turned cold

Cold War memories
they're all I've got
I cannot jettison this baggage
until I meet the faceless one
who haunts me like a ghost

I've seen the thaw a million times in my dreams
I've seen the conflict rage out of control in the past
I want to start to heal the wounds of time
But I don't know how

War in the eighties
equaled isolation in the nineties
How do I express
that an olive branch is what I now hold?
How do I approach the old pain?
How do I let the common enemy know that all is forgiven,
but not forgotten?

Betrayal is a two-edged sword
and it cut us both ways
I tore down the Berlin Wall
but still we're separated
by the polar regions in which we live

Every time I think I've found
the golden years
I create some more
Will you still wage war and ravage the lands?
Will the poor man's atom bomb still suffice
to indiscriminately attack us all?

At one time I spoke proudly
of alliance between nations
of sovereigns who were unafraid
of the consequences of fighting
the erasable minds that thought
we weren't coalitions to oppose

What did we care?
We were writers from different sides of the track
Our universe was the printed page
Let them have the real world
ours was just as good

I burn a candle to this day
and think of how it could have been handled differently

how we could have had it all
Now all I want is to take the first step
to build the future
Can I even lay the first brick?

The Cold War might melt away
The fortresses that were physical are all torn down
but the emotional scars will last
a hundred years more
You can't scale these walls with a pole
You can't batter these doors with a ram
How many times can I rebuild
after the hurricane?

The Cold War was my life
I waged it
when I couldn't speak to my enemy
I chaired subcommittees and debated policies
of annihilation and containment
All the while the commandos plotted their revenge
and the fall of the Republic was only hours away

I can't forget the Cold War
I can't forget the shattered common dreams
I can't forget that at one time I was in charge of the fight
to bring Reaganism to the fore

Don't ask me to explain
I've been haunted by the past too long
I've tried to climb the stairway
but heaven or hell
all I know
is that I was a dreamer
forceful when I wanted to experience something new
If this meant that I would precipitate Armageddon
then damn the consequences

If the truth hurts
I must be the king of pain
One day the police may take me away
but I'll not back up one inch from all that's fit to print
A dreamer's grave means release from the physical
Emotional isolation could end at any time
I'll not let them stop me from achieving all that I can

If only there were time to say all that needs to be said
I'd work up to it like a symphony
but the spark that fires can only be utilized for so long
and if the flame can't burn without oil
it will eventually go out

Can't I end this cold period of war
before it's too late?

THE DEVIL AND THE CIVIL WAR

Many of us go through a period of cleansing our souls, through fires less severe than those of hell, but nonetheless effective in eliminating the vestiges of our previous states of being. What I experienced in the Gulf was a defining influence in my life. A part of me is still out there, trying to recapture the meaning of life that I brought with me, and through that meaning, my outlook on life has changed. In the Persian Gulf I was completely cut off from the world I had known, and it changed immeasurably in the blink of an eye. Warfare evolved out there in those troubled waters, and like it or not, so did the human spirit.

I have wondered whether those who suffer from mental illness are being tormented by the devil in our time, whether we are a troupe of angels or an army of darkness. On the USS *Mobile Bay* I thought that Saddam Hussein, a force of evil, was looking for a being who would make the choices I made, which to my mind made me as good a candidate for the label "Antichrist" as anyone on the planet. If someone living as poor a life as I do can be considered the Antichrist, it shows that the devil will try to capitalize on any situation. But what is true cowardice? Is it bowing out because you don't have the ability to cope with the stresses of a religious conflict? Is it feeling relieved that you were never ordered to kill anyone because you fear what you would become if you did? The devil will hide his true intentions, then let others take the rap for his deeds. Maybe that is true cowardice.

A lot of people believe that the government is "Big Brother" and the New World Order is part of some far-reaching conspiracy. When my shipmates aboard the *Mobile Bay* started acting in ways that made me think there might be some substance to these tales, that's when I jumped into the deep end of the pool. I went through the full spectrum of paranoia, about everything from religious war to sinister government to the vagaries of Saddam Hussein to AIDS to on-board conspiracies to conniving political parties to a resurgence of Communism. The paranoia was fed and driven by books and movies I'd been exposed to, and it led me to believe that if I mentioned something or someone, everyone would either rally for or against me instantly. At one point I actually believed that I would be martyred like Martin Luther King, Jr., or Jesus Christ because of my religious views. When I went to the deck of the ship and saw the fires that Saddam had set in the Gulf lighting up the sky like some eerie view of the end of the world, I began to wonder if we were still in the Persian Gulf, or if we had suddenly been isolated from the entire known world because the government knew there was a battle brewing between Rebels and Unionists on this ship named after a famous Civil War battle.

What would you do if you suddenly saw your home, the internal chambers of a modern warship, turned into a Civil War battlefield? To me the ship was a high-technology war zone for believers and non-believers at the end of the world. If the battle of Revelation was really here, what would you do, suddenly faced with the end of everything? I was mentally fighting a conflict where humanity battled against itself until I could almost hear the Civil War ghosts rising from their graves to give us direction.

In the grip of my delusion I believed that every bit of information was a weapon. Whenever a person said something, I had to evaluate what the message was over and over in my mind. What did that person mean? Why were crewmen on the mess decks yelling personal insults at me? Why did someone turn out the lights as I climbed down the ladder to the next deck? Had the world become angry because I had directed them to play out a scene that no one wanted to experience? I tried to muddle through this paranoid vision, certain that the second Civil War was occurring all around me.

Not everything I experienced on the *Mobile Bay* can be classified as paranoia. There is a line I crossed into abject fantasy, which led to a personal breakdown similar to the meltdown of a nuclear reactor. Faced with a potpourri of the real divisions of people in this world, I began to realize that the Antichrist could use these things to divide us. I firmly believed that, had I not been a devout Christian soul, the old wounds of the American Civil War could have somehow been exploited by such a being to cause the very conflict I wanted to avoid. If those biblical passages aren't referring to past eras, I thought, they must have a vision of what is to come. Prophets have always been demeaned; what if one of them foretells a doom that is true? What if the Virgin Mary has appeared to our Pope and prophesied the way events will occur in this era? What if God knows the future and the past; would he leave things up to chance, or would he send Mary and the saints to make appearances and inform people around the world?

I had to leave the *Mobile Bay* to retain some semblance of stability. I still felt that there were underlying currents of my paranoia that were real. I couldn't allow them to destroy me, and I sought help, just in case this really was the devil's way of playing with someone who might make a difference. If there ever is a physical incarnation of evil and a war against it on this planet, I want to make damn sure the forces of good are victorious. And I know I have a long way to go before I am ready for such a conflict, if it does occur. This is why I'm taking time to assemble my thoughts, to find a way to add, not to cultural paranoia, but to cultural healing. I want this internal battle that I faced to bring out the real issue of the hold paranoia has on us as a nation and as a people. The real questions we need to address are: what is paranoia, what is reality, and how do we deal with it all?

ARE THEY BUILDING THE REPUBLIC?

Does it bother you?
The infrastructure is taken for granted
Roads will always be there
till the day you die

I saw a dozen orange cones along the road
each one at an intersection
On the same road, a sign
"Jesus lives!"
What were they trying to say to me?

In a dazzling delusion
I viewed it all differently
I saw a world
where workmen were soldiers
Instead of wrenches they carried bombs
buried them deep in the earth
and awaited a command to detonate them
to begin a second Civil War

Please tell me is it true
that a billion mines litter our world
Is it true that mines of the mind
are much worse than those
that can take a limb?

Like a toy I picked one up
America's logic said it won't harm me
but it blew me over, knocked me out
That's the last time I tried
to pick up the world

If I'm a revolutionary
lock me up and throw away the key
If I don't believe in mother, child, and family
do I really belong here?
Should I find an unpopulated island
and live like a hermit?
Should I give in to practitioners
to long-dead religion?
A holy war could shake America
Is that what you really want?

Let no one say you blew up the federal courthouse
Let no one say you bombed Centennial Park
Don't be a religious fanatic
or let zealousness tear you away
from ideals for which we all strive
You can care for the lives of the unborn
but don't constrict a life already on this planet
If you mail letter-bombs, don't ask the Lord
"Are you here for me?"

Does it make me human
that I share this room with you?
Does it make me human
that I fight beside you in a war
on the other side of the globe?
Tracers in the night
and oil fields on fire
were the illusions we shared over there.

How could you be so blind to think
the only battle is with a tyrant in the Middle East?
What about illness of spirit and AIDS?
What type of world kills indiscriminately
while ignoring a cure?
And does it really cost too much
to run an environmental world?

If humans really care
about the birds and the fish
then don't spill oil
Draw in the dolphin-safe nets
If you really needed to burn plants and dinosaurs
buy a cabin up in the mountains
show no steam, but burn down the forest
and laugh in glee
You've wrecked our ecology

Big deal, you may say
It's one man's paranoia
The world's gonna live forever
and if I'm gonna die, Christian
I'll take you with me
You think Civil War is your worst nightmare
You haven't seen me!

And the rebels take the hill
and raise the schizophrenic flag
Survey this!
Survey a world where the ideals of man
never bear any fruit
Shoot down the dreamer and his dream
Hunting season has opened again!

It all comes back to the orange cone
If the world wants revenge
if we're polarized
I don't deserve to live with you
nor you with me
Build me a rocket ship to Mars
then you can do what you damn well want with the Earth
but if you're trying to flee the Republic
you'd better stay off the highways

THE FLOODING CASUALTY

It was six years ago that the flood struck Sonar 1 aboard the USS *Mobile Bay* in the Persian Gulf, and in the space of five minutes my life was changed forever. It was this event that prompted the schizophrenic episode that led to my eventual release from naval service during the Gulf War.

That flooding casualty is well remembered by me. I had been ordered to Sonar 1 to conduct routine maintenance, after which I traveled down a ladder to Sonar 4. I was working on various equipment there when I heard a dull booming thud somewhere above me. The lights flickered briefly, and I wondered what had happened. Within seconds I found out, as water started to flood into the room from a plug in the floor.

Amid the rising waters, my first thought was to call the quarter-deck and report the casualty. My second thought was to leave the space before the water created a shock hazard. Going with my first impulse, I quickly relayed my location using the space phone, then felt the door. Since there was no moisture or pressure welts showing, I left as rapidly as I could, climbing the ladder to safety.

As I started my ascent, I heard over the intercom, "Flooding, flooding, flooding in compartment four-one-twenty-four." Although I was climbing rapidly, I noticed moisture running down the door to Sonar 1 as I passed, and water pouring through an unsealed crack at the door's base. I decided to keep climbing to the outside hatch rather than enter Sonar 1. It was a wise choice, as I later learned that there was a definite shock hazard in that compartment. As I reached out to open the exterior hatch, it moved, and I found myself face-to-face with a damage-party crewman who helped me onto the deck. He asked which compartments were flooded; I told him, then immediately went back to Sonar 1 by a different route to check on the progress of the flooding.

By the time I got to the fringe of Sonar 1, a crowd was mulling and the crew was already in the process of pumping water from the space. Someone shut off equipment power to the forward compartments and the emergency lighting came on. I quickly reported to my supervisor what had happened, then tried to lend a hand, but the situation was well under control, as the responding parties knew exactly what to do to keep the flood from spreading.

It was another two hours before the equipment stopped pumping water out of the compartment. I was among the first to enter and survey the damage. It was immediately apparent that the flooding had occurred because a T-valve had given out and exploded into the side of the bulkhead. My eyes opened wide as I realized I had been standing directly in the path of the blowout just three minutes before the valve had given way. A large patch of fiberglass padding behind the spot where my head had been was missing. As I considered this, the remains of the valve were taken away for stress analysis.

It was only after my supervisor had instructed us to clean up Sonar 1 that I began to feel suspicious. One crewman in the party came up with the preposterous claim that I might have had something to do with the explosion. I immediately responded that I had almost been killed by it. He backed off and never ventured that analysis again, but the wheels inside my mind were already turning. Since I was not responsible for the explosion, maybe someone else was. I began to explore every possible rumor of how this casualty had occurred and who may have had the motive and the means to cause it, and I began to see conspiracies everywhere, even under my bunk. I was so delusional that I believed there was a Soviet mole among the crew who had caused the flood to kill a believer in anti-Communism. I started to think that listening devices and pinhole cameras were hidden in each compartment, and it seemed to me that people began to take much more notice of my shipboard movements.

As a result of my response to the casualty I was decorated by the captain, but within two weeks I was in such a delusional state that I had to request a medical transfer to cope with my building illness, an illness that I carry to this day and still battle regularly.

I have come to a couple of solid conclusions in the years since the flooding casualty occurred. The first of these is that I might never have had a trigger moment to start this illness if I hadn't been stationed on the *Mobile Bay* and experienced a shipboard casualty. Another conclusion I've drawn is that I would never have believed a new American Civil War was happening around me if I hadn't been deployed to a ship named after a Civil War naval battle. Also, over the years I have come to feel that God actually guided me to leave that compartment when I did so that I would live to write the books I've written since my military discharge in 1991.

Sometimes a single event can change a person's life—this one certainly changed mine. I am on a very different path today than I was five years ago. Nowhere is this more evident than in my conversion from a far-right anti-Communist to an open-minded centrist. Only time will tell if I'm a better person for the things I've experienced. One thing is certain: My life took a radical turn during the years of my recuperation. I am a far different person today than I might have been if I had stayed on board the USS *Mobile Bay*.

THE AMERICAN CIVIL WAR, PART II

A Civil War is a hard thing to swallow
Off the coast of Iraq I felt our time had come
to reestablish history

I worried about the absence of religion
I worried that there was no end
that I would keep replaying the same events
that the Blue and Gray would rise again
Now the American Civil War
haunts a northerner's dreams

What coalitions were active
and which would I follow?
I was a survivalist tackling the toughest issues
Will the next war be about ideas?
Will it be about differences in the way we live?
Isn't the heart of the issue good versus evil
and the extremes to which each will go
to fight the other?

I was the scientist, more than anything
I was an observer
Now I'm a person scorned by my former shipmates
because I needed help, and took a step to leave
a dangerous step

because if the coalitions of my nightmares were real
the pilots assigned to escort me to USS *Comfort*
might have thrown me in the drink
killed me outright or
with or without command's consent
executed me by pushing a button
firing a key to start a missile launch
and I would just then be
another casualty of war

I still recall the shifting vision of leaving mine-watch
and hearing of a security detail being deployed
in passageways I had to travel to get back to my bunk
They were there to protect the weapons of the ship, not me
this much I knew
but they were armed with loaded weapons
and in my state of mind
it seemed that any gun could be fired by an unauthorized user
and they were blocking my path to the only home I knew
I stayed topside, immobilized,
until I heard a voice over the intercom
It said, "All clear"

Dumping trash at night was far easier
but when I saw the cigarette extinguished
as I opened the hatch
I knew there was a leap of trust I could not make
I knew that I couldn't trust that illicit smoker
to allow me to work unhindered
and if I fell off a ship in the middle of the night
who would have tried to save me
amid the poisonous sea snakes
and the darkness of the war zone
And if I fell in and swam to shore
my only point of entry
would be the coastline of Iraq in the distance

I have observed seas before a storm
and the skies and dolphins and the patterns of birds
but nothing prepared me for being on a ship
which seemed on the brink of Civil War

I heard weird messages
"Dixie" playing on the intercom
a shipmate singing a Civil War song
and the Blue and the Gray weren't just teams on the
flight deck
they were everywhere

Who could I trust
I was a waif deployed as a dishwasher in the galley
and Saddam's rhetoric poured into my ears
from dawn to dusk

Do your duty, they said
but what was that?
There were no submarines in the Gulf
nor was there much else to do
but clean the rising stacks of used food pans and utensils
Was this reality?
Were they trying to force me
to clean these pans, still filled with food
to make me a mark, easily located
for quick elimination in any conflict for the ship?

When battle is enjoined
whom will you follow?
Who will be your guiding force
your philosophy of life
as the knives of war are drawn and sharpened?

Caesar in the senate
could not have felt such paranoia

It seemed I was at Earth's end
I felt we were no longer on the planet
Did no one else have this feeling
of being in purgatory?

By day I could hear
booming guns shoreward
mines exploding in the water
fires raging out of control
shipboard compartments flooding
dead soldiers floating in the water
a funeral service for our enemy that no one would accept

By night I could see the coalition aircraft flying on missions
By night America and the world might cease to exist
Fear was my companion on this journey
and I had nowhere to go, no escape
all I could do was let my fear and distrust
ravage my mind unchecked

Niagara Falls was the message of my deliverance
from this internal hell into which I had descended
The message was painted and said time and time again
that I must believe I am important enough
to be saved

I thought the hour of deliverance was at hand
when a member of the crew told me
to gather my things and leave the ship
Instead I walked into officers' country
and although this alerted them
of the mind games I had experienced
I was too far along the path of my internal turmoil
to remain an active member of the crew

I thought that an overt battle
was raging all over the ship
It was at that time that a separation occurred
I thanked Dave for having me on board
I was loyal only to him and to the captain
But even as we spoke the lie that I was leaving for a few days
I knew I'd never be back

St. Jude had it rough
but he died from his injuries
and although his suffering was localized and particularly acute
he didn't have to live with what might have been
if he had followed a different path
He suffered and died, but I'm left here
with the faded fire of my own intoxication
with the concept of the Civil War

ISOLATION

When isolation is consistently forced on an outsider it can make him into a reactionary person, or someone the world doesn't want or need, like those who commit crimes against humanity. But there are other kinds of outsiders, such as the category into which I fit myself—the outsider who cares deeply about such things as nuclear proliferation, hunger, and justice, who sees the consequences of believing that greed is the only religion to pursue, and who tries to make sure that future generations will exist, so that at the end of time the human race might span the universe.

When I was aboard the *Mobile Bay* I was a loner, and I had to keep much of the conflict I was experiencing to myself. But as my condition worsened, I became a target for many of the crewmen. During my breakdown, when word got around about my illness, I was given the worst dressing-down by my shipmates that I had ever witnessed. The crew used every derogatory term they could think of to try and incite this stricken member of their crew to some outlandish action. They tore my belongings when I wasn't watching, and on one occasion someone verbally threatened my life. I felt like Daniel in the lion's den. Even during my trip back from the Gulf, I faced evil-minded people who seemed to be testing my reactions, hoping for some entertainment.

Since my breakdown on the *Mobile Bay* the few friends I thought I'd made there have refused to talk to me. I've tried to open up a new dialogue with many of them, but they never respond to my communications. If I were still experiencing paranoid delusions, I would believe that people were not responding because they belonged to organizations trying to control the world. But I realize now that they are as afraid to touch this issue as I once was. I realize that forgetting and forgiving might take some time, but I am hopeful that, eventually, they will try to reach out and repair these channels with me, and not shun me because of an illness I couldn't control.

In the Circles of Command

In the circles of command
my case was tossed around
and laughed off the cuff
It was only through prudence
of naval principals
that anything got done

At the lower levels
enlisted men said
"Why bother, rough him up
injure him for the record"
It was only command directive
that agreed
to let me go peacefully

My driver to the presidio
was very forthcoming with threats
He picked me up at the airport
and to the others he said
"Let's dump the stiff on the road and make him walk"
and everyone knew who he meant

Two people visited Niagara Falls from Olendorf
They wanted to know if a fight had broken out on the *Bay*
Were there any broken bones to mend?

They quickly disappeared
when the subject of Civil War
turned out to be only in one man's mind

Describe a scene of tension so thick
you could cut it with a knife
As I walked through officers' country
I saw a gun pointed at another ship
I didn't know what to say or do

The journal I'd kept on board
did not prepare me
for a meeting with the XO
I discussed quite candidly the fact
that a Civil War was brewing
on the pages of my mind

HM2, HM1, none had a clue
how to handle this case
of a man who couldn't even wash his clothes
because those ordered to show him the way
didn't show up

I grabbed the gold and silver, too
I wasn't going to leave wealth behind
There was no telling who I'd face
when I got back to my locker
If gold were God
there were many whose religion
was the happy medium
the alloy to save your life in a crisis
The theme of man, my thesis of life
is that you can only trust your fellows so far

I left the literature for warlords to find
if they did indeed inhabit the ship

Let them battle for turf
Let them do it right or wrong
Let them be Exhibit A
in my defense for believing
the score was Civil War six, Crew none
The time on the clock said 1861

TM1 was master-at-arms
then one day reinforcements arrived
and on the same day promotions flew
What was an apprentice of the initiate to think
Let God strike them dead if they dealt wrongly
with a person who only saw surfaces
while serving on the *Bay*

The command tried to figure out
why a person would react this way
They tried to let sense sink in
by giving me a cap to take to the bridge
There was no Civil War, just men working
but I couldn't see it
through the garbage programming I'd seen and read
for many a moon up to that day

Civil War or laughing stock
"Let's berate the bringer of foreboding"
My thoughts are crystal clear
about the real malevolent attitudes of men
They thought I'd do something stupid for them
Stupidity cuts both ways
because at the end
Civil War was closer to reality
than anyone would believe
If they wanted to play with fire
children could easily torch the house

I apologize, sir Captain
if I've brought the NIS down upon your ship
to scour your crew
on a witch hunt for a Civil War
that was my christening of sorts

I was only searching for deeper meaning
I wanted an understanding of events
that matched the wisdom of my years
Instead I've got the fire
of a religious battle that won't die
Scorched and flaming, falling debris
All I can do
is hide under a table in the basement
and hope the meteor
doesn't strike me where I lay

Bravery can be foolhardy
and fools abound in Tinseltown
I'm just a man whose message
has never been clearer
I can only navigate nebular extremes for so long
before I must reinvent myself

If only I was a firebrand
a flame of vicious, righteous causes
I would throw myself
on the bringers of stigmata

I found the dunce in an elevator
He was black
but he still wore the sheet of a racist
unleashed on the town

Women, hide your food
and hide your children young and old

Let the bringers of pain seek their suppers elsewhere
If I were the innkeeper I'd burn the house down
before letting in their like

Desert Storm or Desert Thorn
I've met a desert full of buffoons
Let me understand exactly what you've said
behind your veil of legal mumbo jumbo
"It's time," said the president, "to unleash the viper
and draw some blood"

Whether VA, DON, or DOD
Treasury, FBI, or BATF
when they come for you, you'll know
the Republic has no religion
but itself!

THE
ROAD BACK

SHADES OF PARANOIA

Whether it is the distorted voices
that make the most peaceful passages
contain the worst blasphemy
Whether it is nearly being run down by a police car
or wanting Superman to fly me away
from a destiny that seems shattered
into a million pieces
paranoia keeps it coming

The sounds of settling furniture
cause the mind's eye
to believe in a battle
between angels and devils

The streetlights tell a tale of electricity
Where blackout means eclipse of the spirit
and lighted means we follow the golden path

I close my eyes
and suddenly
I am a member of the elite
Put your hopes and dreams in my hands
and I'll take away the suffering of millions

Paranoia, I cannot forget
living on the edge
on the brink, with a tracer fired
to track the progress of the mind
back from the brink, now inspired

Get the delusion in print
suffer the derision and scorn for a bit
so that you can test the waters
Is humanity ready
for the schizophrenic author?

ONE MAN'S FIGHT

I was first diagnosed with schizophrenia in 1991. Since that traumatic time I have spent many hours soul-searching, trying to adjust to my illness and put my life back together. I have not always been successful. It is an ongoing quest to understand my disease and to come to terms with it.

The schizophrenia from which I suffer is characterized by delusions of grandeur and a strong feeling of persecution by members of society in general. Random destructive events, such as my parents' car being torched by an arsonist or the theft of a pair of audio speakers that I owned, can cause me to believe that there is an organized plot against me. Confrontations and fights that I witness seem to indicate that one of the participants has sided with my views of the world and is being attacked by the other element of society. To a schizophrenic with my symptoms, worries about my own personal safety cause me to be suspicious of any friendly person or voice. When I encounter a person with an aggressive nature, my fears are even greater. Simple conversations that I overhear on the street may be interpreted by my mind as a real and viable threat. The way a person says something to me, or the gestures he or she uses, can become a virus on my mind which, if not counteracted by medication, will make me so sick that I can no longer be a functioning member of society.

When I first learned from a Veterans Administration (VA) doctor that I had this disease, my initial reaction was strong denial. I refused to believe that my mental state wasn't exactly as it should be. I denied that I had a problem. And although I dutifully took the allotted medication (haloperidol and Cogentin), I was fearful of accepting the fact that I had come down with a disease as misunderstood and stigmatized as schizophrenia.

Once I was released from the VA medical system I immediately stopped taking my medication. I was so embarrassed to have this disease that I refused to tell anyone of my condition. The longer I remained off the medication, the more my outlook on life darkened.

I suffered my first and only relapse in 1992. In the delusional state of this relapse, my mind took every bit of fantasy and science fiction to which I had ever been exposed and thrust it all into a living patchwork of threats against my being. Movies such as *Blade Runner* and *Total Recall* became "science fact" to me. I felt like I was living a dangerous fantasy life. This, in conjunction with flashbacks to my combat experience in the military, soon had me believing that I was in some serious race to save society from itself. I believed during this time that I was carrying secret documents inside my head that were dangerous to the state, and I cannot even begin to describe to you how justified I felt in every defensive action I eventually took. It was ultimately a simple flat tire on my motorcycle (which also seemed a part of a conspiracy) that convinced me that I truly needed help.

I was readmitted to the Veterans Administration medical system in May of 1992. The VA hospital reconnected me to my supply of medication, for which I am eternally thankful. However, I discovered that I was thrust into a category of "mentally incurable individuals."

These people exhibited a wide range of mental disorders, and the hospital acted as nothing more than a caretaker for their bodies, as if to say to all of these forgotten souls, "Be as sick as you want to be, we can't fix what ails you." For the first month of my stay I took that adage to heart. I refused to seek the help I needed, and I feared and loathed any attempt made to help me come to terms with my illness. It was only when I realized that I might be forced to spend the rest of my life in the company of eternally suffering individuals (patients, staff, and doctors included) that I finally started to change my life for the better. I made it my mission to seek the help I needed and to effectively stay out of the VA medical system as much as possible. I am eternally grateful that the VA was there for me when I needed it, however, and I hope one day to repay them for the favor they did in rescuing me from this illness' worst effects before it was too late.

Since then I have recovered from my illness. By looking at me or observing my actions over a period of time, it might be difficult to determine that I suffer from schizophrenia. But I know that if I don't take my current dosage of haloperidol, I will very quickly be back in the state of mind that makes it difficult for me to function in society.

There are risks involved in taking my medication. One documented side effect is that it can cause vision problems in the short term, and another is that an involuntary movement disorder can occur if it is taken over an extended period of time. I am willing to risk suffering these side effects for the benefits my medication currently produces in my life. Really, I have little choice. Either I take the medication and live a life where I can occasionally contribute something to society, or I suffer the delusions and paranoia associated with my disease. Given that, who wouldn't choose to recapture a more stable life? The fact that I have returned to school and am studying for a degree is a tribute to the effectiveness of my treatment.

Once I thought that schizophrenia only happened to other people, but I'm living proof that this disease strikes down even some of the hardiest of veterans. I have learned that schizophrenics need a lot of help and concern to live a normal life. If they don't have a good support system, they might wind up in perpetual states of darkness, completely unable to function, to go to work and raise families. It is by promoting a better understanding of things such an afflicted person has to offer society that I can exorcise some of the demons that have plagued me for a long time.

REBUILDING

A dreamer, I climbed the walls of the Republic
I chased you, elusive one
to find out if you existed
to see whether the Republic turned a blind eye
to all the things that were wrong

Who's braver?
A man who is pushing the envelope of the mind
or societies with nuclear-tipped comments
pointed at each other?
Dear world, why do you let fools
call me on the phone
to ask me whether a man with a birthmark on his head
is leading the world to ruin?

In my quiet desperation
one thought keeps coming through:
to gain acceptance
for fighting the battle
Let the world credit me for rebuilding
on a foundation of shattered stones
Let us all believe that even the lowest born
can one day be
a king among men.

FROM INSIDE THE VA SYSTEM

1 September 1996

I am now one of the meek in this lifetime, a person who has suffered through mental illness and is trying to come back and write about my most traumatic fear—a second Civil War in America. You can say that I'm still suffering from the illness by admitting this, but I must tell you that I feel this latent conflict may come into focus at the end of this era.

This proclamation might shake the Republic to its foundation; then again, people might just laugh it off as the ramblings of a schizophrenic. Obviously, I am not strong enough to be the bringer of doom for the American people. But I do know that Saddam Hussein unleashed this message far more than I.

I believe that the evil in this world is focused to reignite the American Civil War and/or create a police state. I want to prevent this. So many films are focused on this theme, and they all have some basis in reality. While I admit I have this disease, that doesn't diminish the fact that movies like *Total Recall* describe a conflict that actually exists in our society.

There could be a terrible war at some point in our future. That is what I'm trying to get across to the generations in this age. This could be the one battle that affects humanity more deeply than any other. If World War III is fought, the heart of the issue will be a conflict far worse than people imagine, a conflict of the spirit that will echo throughout our world for all eternity.

All of humanity is important, not just a portion of it or a particular race. We are all human. I am a person who has been wrestling with some of humanity's toughest issues. This is the reason I have come to this confrontation with evil, and now I might draw more attention from the dark forces at work in our world because I have announced myself as a researcher of this conflict. If I come into any power to influence the minds of our citizens, my conflict with the dark forces will grow. The "Dark Side of the Force" isn't just some techno-babble from *Star Wars*—it's as real as the conflict between good and evil.

I fear becoming the direct messenger of this conflict, because I don't have the necessary confidence to present the issue to our world—not yet. If there were confidence-enhancing drugs I could take that would make me into a fearless warrior for humanity, I might be able to take on this responsibility. But I know full well that drugs are a part of the illness affecting humanity. I aim to cure that disease along with all the other wide-ranging problems that none of our leaders are willing to face unless they consider them useful political issues.

There are so many signs that I see. An example is the sightings of Mary in this age. I believe that she only manifests herself where she knows she can do the most good. I believe she is well aware of what I experienced in the Gulf, and she is reaching people close to me to send the message that she knows what I'm experiencing. Mary only appears to those who are strong enough to handle a visitation, just like UFO phenomena are only reported by those with the constitution to effectively handle the unknown. I pray that she will have the confidence in me to guide my quest and strengthen my spirit.

I would not doubt that high-ranking members of the Catholic Church have been visited by Mary. The Catholic Church knows my struggle better than I do myself. They know what has transpired and the significance of those events. They are keeping their distance because they are in denial as much as I am about this conflict—no one wants to believe they are living in the last days before Judgment. I also don't doubt that some of the highest members of the Roman Catholic Church are holding documents on people who might have an impact on us as we head into the next century. You can be sure that behind the scenes, my name and information are being stored in political arenas as well as at the Vatican.

Regarding UFO phenomena, my research has left me with a lasting opinion that whatever conflict is fought on this planet will be actively supported by alien forces. I believe, based on what I already know about the conflict, that these forces already support factions on Earth. Be prepared to face your worst fears, and the unknown, if this conflict comes to pass. If there is another war—the Armageddon of the Bible—then only your wits and intelligence and the hand of God will help you survive it. Be prepared to see technology and techniques that have never been seen before if that battle occurs in this age.

I am a messenger that has seen the start of a fire, a lit fuse that will engulf our world if we don't do something about it. My problem is that I was unprepared to deal with this issue aboard the USS *Mobile Bay*, and I must grow and sort out my problems so that I can effectively involve people in this conflict before evil has had a chance to marshal its forces in this world. My life has been one of intensive isolation, and I doubt there is a cure for the disease of spirit that ails me, but I am sure as hell not going to take my own life because the system can't cure the illness from which I suffer.

My conflict is still unresolved, but I know the forces that are at work in this world far better than I ever did before. I recognize that I need to find some way to recover from this illness so I can serve humanity in this age. My fight against evil is real, and this disease is real. But I don't know how much longer I will be able to write about this issue without the disease shaking me to my very essence.

WERE THE PARANOIA REAL, HOW FAR WOULD IT GO?

In the darkest corners
of a mind on the blink
aliens invade or subvert
angels and demons battle
plagues are loosed from laboratories
nukes fly and hit towns, cities, and homes
races battle for supremacy of the Republic
Big Brother watches over us
Mother Nature fights back against polluters and rapists
and the Second Coming seems simplistic beside it all

Civil War logic
pervades the mind
and makes you realize
how fragile life really is on this planet

If we fight a third World War
everything is fair game
everything from our past can be used again
every crazy philosophy will reign
and no one will oversee it all

We've seen the Church in control
we've seen plagues and barbarians
we've seen pirates and fires and floods
What we haven't seen is the unification of our race

If there was truly an evil-minded being
he could arrive and control the human race
he could hide his true intentions so easily
and he could manipulate people's minds

It's Civil War logic
I didn't ask to be exposed
to so much paranoia
I only went on a search for the truth
but when you view too many sides
you can lose yourself

Every element of fantasy
fuels the struggle
Do you want a world of science or magic
an economic miracle or ESP
astronomy or astrology
a religious prophet, black or white
flying motor cars or alien craft
Do we want a cure for the diseases of man
or food on the table and a loving family?
A society where computers serve us or control us
or annihilate us?

If the symbolism becomes overt
either the end is near
or coalitions are recruiting talent
The next war is purely good versus evil
Let them worry about the symbolism
of science fiction or fantasy
All I ask is to not believe my mind's eye
when it told me
that the jokers in the defense department
don't have a clue

The Civil War is a gaping wound
a hole that could divide us forever

it's American-made schizophrenia
Is it any wonder it drew me in?

When too much is at stake
do I sit back like the government
laughing at all the deviants
we failed to properly educate?
People following the material god
laugh at the spiritual man
He doesn't care for a job or money
He just wants to live as a free man

My dream is that I'll find a new world
that doesn't cut us down
where dreams are safe
as safe as the streets we walk
They're all lit up and paved with intentions of gold
and the pictures I see in the newspaper
are the way things really are

Schizophrenia is the backwater
it's the preserve where dreamers are held
but I'm just not sure at this stage
whether there ain't an element of truth
to all the paranoia I've seen

FEARS AND VISIONS

When I was hospitalized at the VA hospital in Marion, Indiana, in 1992, I believed I was experiencing the last days of persecution on Earth and that the Civil War virus I had carried back from the Gulf had infected everyone around me, forcing them to take North-South positions on every issue. I thought that the American Civil War, phase two, was beginning, and that I had been the catalyst. My reaction was so pronounced that I sat in that VA hospital for two days, shaking my head sadly as if to say, "What have I done?" My condition wasn't helped by the fact that many of the people sharing the ward were in states of mind far worse than my own.

During the following days of my hospitalization I almost lost control of my mental state permanently. After sitting with my hands cupped on the table, shaking my head to and fro, a new phase of my illness occurred where I retreated deep into my mind. Twice I found myself slowly walking towards the exit door to the on-staff doctors' offices and realized I had almost no control over my movements. The door was open on both occasions, and the staff had to scramble to shut it, fearful as they were that I might harm a doctor. But I was viewing this entire incident from some far-off corner of my mind, as though I was sleepwalking while awake. I think it was a subconscious decision by my mind to get my body to walk as a way of resetting my internal metabolism so I could fight the illness again. I was suffering a severe relapse at that point.

When I began to regain my mental stability, I started to notice the signals that the staff used to warn each other that a patient might become violent. The ward was locked off from a control room, which was always manned so a staff member could call for help if it was needed. The VA staff were always concerned with potential violence, because they were under-funded and understaffed. I realized that if the Civil War occurred in the hospital, as I thought it would on several occasions, they would probably have to let the problem burn itself out, as happens during riots in a prison. This was a constant fear, but one that never came to pass. Once when I was prescribed the wrong medication, I started to hear horns like the angel Gabriel's and screaming that had no rational source. I felt there was a battle for control of my mind being waged, and that I was on trial for all of humanity. It seemed like I was mentally and physically fighting the devil tooth and nail to retain control. Every fairy tale and fable I'd ever been exposed to suddenly took on a darker meaning, and every movie seemed to be about good versus evil. My apartment became a battleground for heaven and hell. I heard neuron clickings and stomach rumblings inside my body, and snaps and settling noises that accentuated every point I was trying to understand about this terrible conflict. I even felt that the Internet was established to give the forces of good and evil a new forum for communication.

When you're exposed to paranoia for too long, you start to believe in its reality, and it's a tough road to get back. On board the *Mobile Bay* I tried to cope with too many stressors at once, and I paid the ultimate price for letting my problems build up to a climax the way they did. This has forever changed my life, as I have had to experience a seemingly endless series of paranoid delusions in an effort to get back to the picture of the world that I had before that time.

Many people who suffer from schizophrenic disorders are so far down a path of deterioration that they cannot express their visions and their fear. Exploring my own path has been a strange and difficult journey. Now, at least, I have a deeper understanding of some of the things I experienced along the way.

PRESIDIUM, I WALKED YOUR LAND

Fireworks in the cathedral
A wide open backyard
Whether they were real or make-believe
they had an effect
on a mind recovering
from the vestiges of intoxication
with itself

I mixed the blues and blacks
with the whites
humor was my concoction
ignorance my quarter
that I put in the machine

Colorful, though
this mess I've wrought
Weird the reasons why
I stay up half the night
to sort the shades of my life

A curtain blocks out my revelation
of a life imperfect and impure
of a chaser of cars and lights
of a dog avoiding the avalanche
to bring the brandy back

to the house of a master who deserted him
six years ago

The darkness calls out
with voices from the past
but in the daylight we visit amusement parks
and laugh and scream
Carry on, wayward soul
I'll meet you by the movie theater at six
This base, soon to be closed
in a harbor of a western land
is still alive in my mind

I carried the future
in an old sock
white as day
and full of the belongings
of a man who believed
he could influence an important mind
at the edge of time

Six years have passed
and now I'm at the crossroads
of personal growth
It took thirty years to build the pyramids
It's taken me twice as long
to build the roads
that Tom Spiece regularly travels

You may not want me around
on the next part of the journey
There'll be hell to pay
if I arrive at my destination
The life I've led
and the consequences of the event
don't add up to the price I'll pay

I'm exploring the last frontier on this planet
How far must a mind go
before it returns
How do I step
back over the line
What does it all mean?

My mind is clearer now
than it was before
in the mental state that punished me
every time I admitted
I've got an incurable disease

The military was the source of this disorder
a gift for a sailor living on the harlequin
I can no longer laugh as freely as before
I only wonder
if the Philippine dream I once lived
was real
or if I will forever be searching the world
for my lost dreams?

CONCLUSION

I have not always been right in every view I've held in life, but I do know that not everything I've seen can be summed up as paranoid delusion. America lives in a fantasy world as much as I do. From sports to movies and television, this culture thrives on fantasy, much of it paranoid. You need go no further than the surface to see the symbolism. If you start to put a label on *The Wizard of Oz* as a Republican idea because Dorothy is from Kansas and so is Bob Dole, then you can see into the deeper end of the pool. I looked profoundly into the paranoia of the American consciousness when I was on the *Mobile Bay*. I have come to the conclusion that the culture we live in has caused my illness as much as anything I have said or done myself. If it regressed further into barbarism, we would be in danger of causing our extinction as a race.

My own process of revelation has shown me that my worst nightmare is a cultural breakdown leading to a schism far worse than one fueled by politics. This conflict, I fear, would go to the very core of humanity. As a person researching the problems of our race, I need more time to try to diagnose the ailment of spirit that affects humanity in our time. Nothing about this new phase of my life is going to be easy. But I'm more dedicated to creating a world in which I can be proud to be a member, a world where everyone is given the chance to offer new ideas on the questions that have plagued our finest minds, and of promoting a community of mankind that doesn't laugh at those of us who are different, but accepts and welcomes diversity. It's important that we all stick together—as a country, as a world, and as a race.

In my quest to broaden my views about the true scope of the struggle I perceive on this planet, I have made mistakes and followed dead ends that I should have ignored. Every time, I get a little bit closer to the truth, but I still don't have all the answers, and probably never will. All I can do is try to leave my mark so that others will know that I've lived and that my life on this planet has meant something. God gave me a chance to make a contribution to the world, and I am going to do my best to make it.

HEALING

I don't ask forgiveness
I've done nothing wrong
All I ask is that you listen
to one man in combat
in the corridors of the mind
one man who'll break through
to the other side
and tell the world what it's like
to suffer an illness of the mind

Only time will tell if you'll listen
I'm no longer afraid of this branch of the unknown
Life is living, making mistakes
and learning not to make them again
If growth can bring me back from the brink
shouldn't the survivors all agree
that it's better to be alive?

Mobile Bay, let us forgive
we survived the war on different levels
but I'll never forget what you put me through
as I searched for the truth in those days

I want to be a part of the future
whatever it may hold
I can't go on as a prisoner
chained to a radar site
I've got to leave Iraq behind

Tell me that you still believe in
humanity's dream
Look up at the sky
The dream's still there
Can I encourage you to pursue it
before I have to die?

EPILOGUE

AFTERWORD

Every life has a thousand stories, if not a million of them. All of the things we do are a part of experiencing what life has to offer. In my lifetime I have escaped death by an eyelash, I have sat in the eye of a hurricane, I have survived the right of passage from childhood to becoming a young man, I have visited the ends of the Earth, and I have enjoyed victory and suffered defeat too many times to count. I have been the outsider all my life; I have been the person courting disaster. I have been a true rebel, too proud to go to the high school graduation or prom. I have been very dedicated, always doing my job to the best of my ability, whether it was delivering papers or paint, driving, or searching for submarines. I have accepted and rejected religion at different stages of my life. I have followed the conservative movement of the Reagan era to my own personal crescendo in the Persian Gulf. I have been ever the idealist in a generation seemingly devoid of any motive other than profit. I have been drawn to anti-Communism, physical fitness, baseball, and getting the most enjoyment out of every moment of life, all in one breath. Ever since I was exposed to the Bible and the book of Revelation, I have feared Armageddon, both personal and worldwide, and have tried to armor myself for its eventuality.

Through all of these experiences, I have always dreamed of becoming the crime fighter who would never give up, the hero who would cleanse this nation of all of the violence, gangs, drugs, and other destructive elements that have swamped our nation in the modern era. This dream has kept me alive during my worst trials, and helps me to live a life that I can believe in. If I can always find a quiet place to dream and gain inspiration, I will always find the strength to continue the struggle.

From the edge of reality, one man still dreams . . .

EAST RACE
(A PRAYER)

Down by the East Race Waterway
is a place where I can reach out to Jesus,
the Holy Spirit, and the Lord

The East Race Waterway
has always been my home
I see my vision, my understanding of things
by watching waters flow
Divide so high, currents so strong
the split in the world can be readily seen
by peering into dark waters
that tell the tale of the other side

Frozen or rainy
I always seem to make it back
I catch the message of trout jumping high
and I can look up into the sky for guidance
regardless of the regiment
I've set for myself

Once, at the edge of dawn
I asked for revelation, and got it
The process of becoming an author
just takes some time
as the river flows under and around
the works of man

Halfway frozen
I made my way to the spot I'd chosen
to call for help, to right this ship
It seemed the world had gone mad
The river called out
and I heard the raging
my ragged cry for a way
out of the valley of darkness

The East Race is a state of mind
a corner of reality
where I can compose my thoughts
to write this next line
Standing by Antarctic waters
I can see clearly
the mysteries they hold
and strengthen my ideal
of not seeing the river's dreams
snuffed out like a candle
before the harshest winds

Raceway, if I leave you for a moment
hold vigil till the return of my seeing eye
that covers the globe, spans time
sees lost loves
and those never to be
Let me meet the dreamer within
Let me find calmer waters
Let me be with you here in spirit
to lighten our plainclothesman's gait
as we tread the corridors of a city
from the vantage of the peninsula

In your absence I can still dream
of finding your equal
You were the first of the unconquerable dreams
and simple minds would never understand

that the beauty of knowing of you
was only sidetracked
by knowing the pedestal was an island
in the middle of a harbor
I am weary and poor
but I'd swim the English Channel
if I could find someone down to earth
who is so fine

Raceway, vanish all my cares
court a flooding disaster
and at the end of the journey
let me know you're still there
Scatter the ashes of the fallen
both North and South
Purify the quest
and let me never lose the courage
to seek your wisdom
whether in peace or war

LEGEND   THE FOLLOWING ABBREVIATIONS WILL BE USED IN GAIN ENTRY AND LOSS ENTRY COLUMNS

GAINS

ENL	- ENLISTED	RECDP	- RECEIVED DRILL PAY
REEN	- REENLISTED	RECNP	- RECEIVED NON PAY
EXTENL	- EXTENDED ENLISTMENT	RECTREAT	- RECEIVED FOR TREATMENT
RECACDU	- RECALLED TO ACTIVE DUTY	RECCFO	- RECEIVED IN CONNECTION WITH FITTING OUT
RECACDUTRA	- RECEIVED FOR ACTIVE DUTY FOR TRAINING		
RECDUT	- RECEIVED FOR DUTY	LOSSES	
RECTAD	- RECEIVED FOR TAD		
RECTD	- RECEIVED FOR TEMPORARY DUTY	RELACDU	- RELEASED FROM ACTIVE DUTY
RECTEMDUINS	- RECEIVED FOR TEMPORARY DUTY UNDER INSTRUCTION	RELACDUTRA	- RELEASED FROM ACTIVE DUTY FOR
RECDUINS	- RECEIVED FOR DUTY FOR UNDER INSTRUCTION		TRAINING
RECTADUINS	- RECEIVED FOR TEMPORARY ADDITIONAL DUTY	DISCH	- DISCHARGED
	UNDER INSTRUCTION	TRAN	- TRANSFERRED

1 TYPE AND DATE OF GAIN ENTRY	2 ACTIVITY	3 DUTIES	4 TYPE AND DATE OF LOSS ENTRY	5 INITIALS A	B
ENL 26 OCT 87	MEPCOM	RECRUIT	TRAN 26 OCT 87	BLP	BLP
RECTEMDUINS 26 OCT 87	CRUITRACOM, NTC, SAN DIEGO, CA.	RECRUIT TRAINING	TRAN 88 Jan 20	BLP	PLC
RECTEMDUINS 20JAN88	FLEASWTRACENPAC, SDIEGO	STUDENT	TRAN 06APR88	BN	JK
RECTEMDUINS 07APR 88	ESG, ES3,	STUDENT	TRAN 29JUL88	DA	MB
RECDUINS 29JUL88	FLEASWTRACENPAC SAN DIEGO CA	STUDENT	TRAN 08SEP89	SA	RMC
RECTEMDUINS 89SEP14	FLEMINWARTRACEN CHARLESTON, SC	RATE OF: STG3 STUDENT	TRANS		
ECTEMDUINS 90FEB10	FLEASWTRACENLANT NORVA BY PSD NAVSTA NORFOLK VA	STUDENT OF RATE: STG3	TRAN 15JUN90	BMK	BMK
RECTD 90JUN16	TPU NAVSTA SAN DIEGO CA BY PSD NAVSTA SAN DIEGO CA	TRANSIENT OF RATE: STG3	TRAN 23 Jun 90	JAM	JAM
RECDUT 90JUN23	USS MOBILE BAY (CG-53) PACFLT/ YOKOSUKA JAPAN	SDCD: 90 JUN OF RATE: STG3	TRAN 8 MAR 91	HH	G

No FURTHER ENTRIES

NAME (Last, First, Middle)	SOCIAL SECURITY NO	BRANCH AND CLASS
		USN

(TC-SD-1070/10 in lieu of NAVPERS 1070/605 (REV. 3-80)

5

● GAIN	2. ACTIVITY	3. UIC	4. LOSS	5. INITIALS GAIN	LOSS
TEMDU 91MAR08	NAVAL HOSPITAL OAKLAND PATIENTS BY PSD OAKLAND CA	31649	TRAN 91JUL03		AMB
TEMDU 91JUL03	TPU TI SFRAN CA	31746	TRF	EBG	EBG
TEMDU 91JUL03	TPU BY PSD TI SFRAN CA 94130	31746	TEMP RET 91SEP20		
91 NOV 199	NRFC NOLA (RECORDS ONLY)		DISCH 30SEP91		mm
●					
●					

NAME (Last, first, middle initial)	SOCIAL SECURITY NUMBER	RANK/RATE
VIDUKA, ALLEN GENE		STG3/E4